CAREERS *in Your Community*™

WORKING
as a
TATTOO ARTIST
in YOUR COMMUNITY

Jason Porterfield

ROSEN
PUBLISHING®

New York

Published in 2016 by The Rosen Publishing Group, Inc.
29 East 21st Street, New York, NY 10010

First Edition

Library of Congress Cataloging-in-Publication Data

Porterfield, Jason.
Working as a tattoo artist in your community/Jason Porterfield.
    pages cm.—(Careers in your community)
Includes bibliographical references and index.
ISBN 978-1-4994-6122-0 (library bound)
1. Tattoo artists. 2. Tattooing. I. Title.
GT2345.P68 2016
391.6'5—dc23

2014046800

Manufactured in the United States of America

Contents

4   Introduction

7   CHAPTER One
     Life in Ink

21   CHAPTER Two
     The Road to Tattoo Artistry

28   CHAPTER Three
     Learning the Trade

39   CHAPTER Four
     Licensing and Standards

50   CHAPTER Five
     The Artist's Life

61   CHAPTER Six
     Opening for Business

68   Glossary
70   For More Information
72   For Further Reading
74   Bibliography
77   Index

Introduction

In the back of a tattoo shop, a man sits somewhat tensely in a dentist's chair while a tattoo artist works over him. She chats with him to put him at ease while she prepares by putting on gloves, and then she shaves the area where the tattoo will go with a disposable razor and cleans it thoroughly with antibacterial soap. She coats the area with alcohol so that she can draw clearer lines. Working quickly and precisely, she uses a stencil to place an outline of the tattoo on the prepared skin.

When she is finished, she checks with the man to make sure it looks right. He confirms the outline, and she starts working. The tip of her tattoo machine dips into a small, disposable capful of ink, and the machine whirs as she applies the ink to the skin. The image takes shape as she changes inks and tips, and she moves from doing the outline to shading and coloring the image, keeping up a steady conversation with the customer. She uses sterile cotton to blot up any blood and ink from the stencil, disposing of the swabs in a biohazard container. When the art is complete, the customer looks it over and agrees that it looks right. The artist, however, is not finished. She gives him a piece of paper with aftercare instructions and tells him how to take care of it and prevent infections. He leaves the shop with new body art that will be with him for a very long time.

Tattooing takes patience, skill, and a steady hand. Here, an artist uses a light and works closely to get her customer's tattoo just right.

Tattoos are a permanent expression of an idea, a memory, or a belief. People may get them to commemorate an important event in their lives or to show their support for a particular cause or dedication to something. They come in shapes as varied as ancient tribal designs and renderings of fine art to symbols representing bands or depictions of film characters. People might get tattoos of religious images, names, or even team logos.

Getting an image permanently placed on one's body is a major commitment. Tattoos can be expensive to have applied, depending on the size and complexity of the design. It can also be costly and difficult to remove them. Finding the right tattoo artist to do the work can be a painstaking process, but becoming an artist takes a much longer commitment. Artists today spend years learning their trade before they even begin to tattoo other people. They study art and artistic techniques. They also learn disease protection and how to keep their customers safe. It is only after they pass tests and receive state licenses that they can begin work.

Many tattoo artists today are skilled and well-trained artists. They work in spotlessly clean studios and closely follow safety standards. These artists serve as valuable members of their communities. Their shops are often gathering places where tattoo enthusiasts meet to talk and hang out. They help anchor business districts, bringing customers not only to their own studios but to other shops as well.

CHAPTER One

Life in Ink

Tattoo artists are a direct link to one of humanity's oldest art forms. A tattoo is an image or a pattern created by embedding ink in a person's skin. They take many forms, from simple names or numbers to elaborate designs or reproductions of famous artwork. Religious symbols, cultural icons, and memorials to loved ones are all common designs.

Tattoo artists create these images. Tattoos made thousands of years ago might have been crafted using needles made of bone and inks derived from berries. Modern tattoo artists use sophisticated instruments and pigments designed to be put into the skin safely. They follow safety standards and guidelines that would have been impossible to meet just decades ago. The mainstream acceptance of tattoos has helped tattoo artists move out of the shadows and become respected members of many communities. Their skills, their talents, and the profitability of their shops have opened many eyes to the value of this ancient art form.

A tattoo parlor sits among stores selling shoes, clothing, and souvenirs in London's popular Camden Town shopping district. Such studios help draw tourists to the area.

Tattooing in History

Tattooing has a long history that spans many centuries and cultures. Archaeologists have found evidence of tattooing dating back as far as 4,000 BCE in art adorning ancient Egyptian tombs. Evidence just as old has been discovered in Romania. Tattooing instruments such as clay ink pots and bone needles have been found at sites throughout Europe, and some of those artifacts are at least ten thousand years old. In South America, archaeologists have uncovered evidence of tattoos on mummies found in Peru that date back to between 900 and 1350 CE.

Long associated with pagan beliefs, tattoos fell out of favor in much of Europe and were forbidden by religious leaders for several hundred years. All the while, the practice thrived in Native American, Polynesian, and Asian cultures. European explorers who traveled to distant lands sometimes came back with exotic tattoos. Body art became associated with rebellious and defiant attitudes and became

This photograph from the 1880s shows a heavily tattooed member of the Maori, the indigenous people of New Zealand. Tattooing is still an important aspect of Maori culture.

THE ICE MAN'S TATTOOS

The oldest tattoos ever found were discovered by accident in 1991. A pair of hikers traveling through the Austrian Alps found the remains of a man partially frozen in ice. At first they thought it was the body of a skier or hiker who had gotten lost, but it turned out to be a man who died more than 5,200 years ago. Scientists nicknamed him Otzi for the area where he was found and collected a wealth of data from his remains and the tools he carried. They discovered more than fifty tattoos on his body, including on his left wrist, on his legs and feet, and along his spine. The images were simple lines and crosses and had been created by slitting the skin and rubbing charcoal into the cut. Although no one knows the meaning of the tattoos, some scientists have speculated that they were medicinal, as they were placed on parts of the body that were subjected to wear and tear.

The purpose of the many tattoos found on Otzi the Ice Man's body remains a mystery, though they were likely therapeutic. Many of the markings were placed in areas now associated with acupuncture.

popular among people who wanted to distinguish themselves from mainstream society. Many people began associating tattoos with sailors, criminals, and the sometimes dangerous waterfront areas of European port cities.

In the United States, negative associations with tattooing continued from the mid-1800s to near the end of the twentieth century. In addition, tattoo artists were often pushed to the fringes of society. Their studios were seen as unhealthy and undesirable businesses. They were believed to attract crime and contribute to the spread of disease. Beginning in the 1970s, many tattoo artists started working together in an effort to make getting a tattoo safer and to change attitudes about their profession.

Tattooing started to become mainstream in the mid-1990s. In 1992, the Alliance of Professional Tattooists formed to promote safe tattooing practices. As interest in tattoos increased and more people started getting body art, state governments began looking at ways to regulate studios. Many state governments passed laws and set safety standards that closely followed the society's own guidelines. The new emphasis on safety encouraged people who otherwise might not have gotten a tattoo to get one. Today, people from all walks of life have tattoos that express who they are and how they view themselves.

Who Gets Tattoos?

People get tattoos for a number of reasons. Some use body art to mark an important milestone in life, such as the birth of a child. Members of the armed forces sometimes commemorate their service with

One of actress Megan Fox's tattoos is visible at the 2014 Nickelodeon Kids' Choice Sports Awards. It was once rare to see a celebrity with a tattoo.

tattoos, as do police officers, firefighters, and other first responders. Friends may get tattoos together to mark the good times they've had, and members of sports teams sometimes bond by getting tattooed.

Legally, anyone who is age eighteen or older can get a tattoo in any state. Many places also allow teens younger than eighteen to get a tattoo if they have permission from their parents or guardians. However, tattoo studios do have the ability to decide whom they will serve, and many artists will not ink a minor even if the teen has permission. Tattooists understand that what teens like or are interested in when they are seventeen years old might embarrass or bore them when they get older. Ethical artists often encourage teens to wait until they are more mature before they get tattoos.

In the United States, tattoos are acceptable in many walks of life. They are embraced by people across racial, ethnic, and class lines. Actor Johnny Depp, singer Rihanna, actress and writer Lena Dunham, and basketball star LeBron James are just a few of the prominent celebrities whose body art is often on display.

Tattoo artists cater to many different kinds of customers from various age groups and cultural backgrounds. A 2012 survey by the market research firm Harris Interactive found that 21 percent of adults in the United States had at least one tattoo, marking a big increase from 2008, when 14 percent said that they had a tattoo. More women than men said they are tattooed, with 23 percent of women claiming a tattoo compared to 19 percent of men. Responses by age emphasize the changing attitudes toward tattoos. About 38 percent of adults between ages thirty to thirty-nine reported having a tattoo, compared to 20 percent of those ranging in age from twenty-five to twenty-nine and 22 percent of eighteen- to twenty-four-year-olds. About 27 percent of people ages forty to forty-nine reported having a tattoo. Older people were less likely to be tattooed, with only 11 percent of those ages fifty to sixty-four and 5 percent of those ages sixty-five and older having tattoos.

All those millions of people with tattoos were served by a tattoo artist. No one can predict whether tattoos will remain popular for years to come; it is safe to say that much of the social stigma once attached to tattoos has faded and that a skilled artist can make a career out of tattooing. Developing excellent art skills, creating a unique style, and showing an ability to bring a customer's ideas to life while offering friendly, welcoming service are good ways for an artist to guarantee that he or she will stay in demand.

Keeping Up Standards

The days of dirty tattoo studios in seedy parts of town are now part of the past. Tattoo artists today have high standards to meet. They must follow safety regulations that began being introduced only in the 1980s and 1990s. Laws in many states now require artists to receive a certain amount of training before they can go into business.

The professional standards now in place for tattoo artists have helped change views about tattooing. For the most part, tattoo artists have to be educated about sanitary practices designed to prevent contamination and the spread of disease and infection. They need to be able to keep their equipment and their

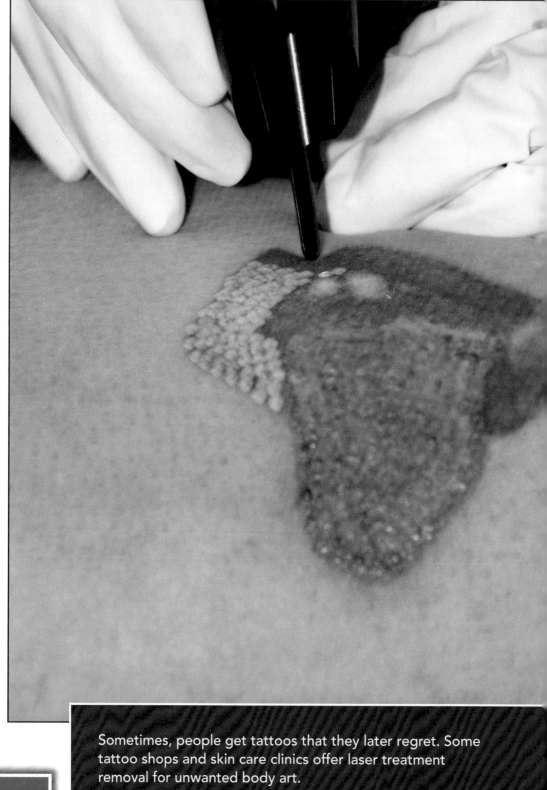

Sometimes, people get tattoos that they later regret. Some tattoo shops and skin care clinics offer laser treatment removal for unwanted body art.

workspace clean and sterile, both for their own safety and for that of their customers. Artists are often required to continue their health safety education even after they receive their license. They might have to take new classes every year or take tests regularly to show that they are staying up to date on preventing illnesses and infections.

Tattoo studios may also encourage artists to continue their art education. Enrolling in higher-level arts classes at local community colleges and even four-year schools can help a tattooist add new skills to his or her repertoire. Many of the best tattoo studios want their artists to be highly skilled and as technically versatile as possible so that they can attract clients who will want to keep coming back. A tattoo artist's success is based on how many clients he or she can bring in. Some artists and studios bring in more clients by offering tattoo removal services or doing custom work to cover up old tattoos.

Tattooing can be challenging work. People train for years before they become certified artists. Some get tired of the work after a few years and switch careers. Others spend their entire professional lives tattooing. Artists don't have many opportunities for career advancement unless they can open their own shop. Instead, they have to focus on building a customer base. Their pay is based on how much their customers pay them. Because they aren't actually employed by a studio's ownership, few tattoo artists receive benefits such as health insurance or vacation time. These expenses have to come out of the artist's own pocket. Artists trade the stability of a guaranteed paycheck and benefits for flexibility.

Part of the Community

When people think of their towns or cities, they may picture a district of shops and businesses near where they live. A city may have several such districts, or a small town may have only a store or two. Public services such as schools, fire departments, and post offices may be part of the mix.

Tattoo studios may not immediately spring to mind for many people, but they are vital parts of many communities. The studio could be in a prominent downtown location, or it might be located on the edge of town. Neighboring shops may be all around. Passersby might pause to peer inside before moving on. If the shop is in a busy location, it's likely that customers will stop at other businesses located nearby before they leave the area.

Many studios offer a wide variety of work and may try to appeal to a very broad audience. This diversification is particularly true in smaller towns where tattoo artists may have to work hard to attract customers from a large geographic area. They attract a broad range of clientele to their shops. Tattoo shops sometimes become a focal point of business activity on a street. Their clients might eat lunch at a restaurant next door or stop in a nearby pharmacy or grocery store to do some shopping, for example.

A successful tattoo artist serves these enthusiasts and the neighborhood as a whole. Tattoo artists

Two young men stand outside a tattoo studio along a prominent stretch of Hollywood Boulevard. The studio is located along the Hollywood Walk of Fame, a popular tourist destination.

encourage their customers to be polite and respect other businesses and deal with those who cause problems. Some tattoo studios—and individual artists—join community organizations such as the local chamber of commerce. This collaboration gives them a voice in planning community events while making them more visible among their fellow business owners. If they make a good impression, they may even change someone's mind about tattooing. Studios also might set up cross-promotional deals with their neighbors, perhaps offering their customers coupons or discounts if they visit another nearby business.

Tattooists also try to be good neighbors by watching out for others in the area. They keep an eye out for any criminal activity or safety issues and report what they see to the proper authorities. If a disaster such as a fire hits an adjacent store, they may pitch in to help with fund-raising or find another way to help. These actions are often appreciated, and other business leaders will remember the friendly tattoo artist who offered help when it was needed.

CHAPTER Two

The Road to Tattoo Artistry

Tattoo artists learn from other tattooists. They spend years perfecting their craft before they even earn a license. Some have formal art training, whether in high school or in college. Others might have nothing more than raw talent and a desire to create lasting images on skin. Some artists have known for years that they want to go into tattooing, while some become interested in the art only after they've grown older and worked in other jobs.

Enthusiasm and Art

Tattoo artists usually start out as tattoo enthusiasts themselves. They love the process of working with a client to get a design just right, from colors and shading to working out the best placement for the art. Feeling a great deal of enthusiasm is important because it makes the artist more likely to create a tattoo that will stand out and make the customer happy. Customers will also be more likely to stick with an

Even experienced tattoo artists draw, sketch, and paint to keep their skills fresh. Here, a tattoo artist works on a new design.

artist who not only does good work but obviously enjoys thinking about and talking about tattoos.

A passion for art and a love of creating images are vital. A tattoo enthusiast who likes looking at and getting tattoos but who hates to draw probably won't make a very good artist. Tattoo artists, particularly those who specialize in custom work, should love to draw or paint. A willingness to experiment with new styles is also important. Being able to create or reproduce works of art in many different styles helps bring in more clients, particularly if the work is done skillfully. Tattooists who do not have formal art training should take classes to learn proper techniques. Those who have taken classes might want to continue their art education to keep their skills sharp.

An aspiring tattoo artist should make it clear that he or she has a real enthusiasm for tattoos. Many artists don't decide that they want to become tattooists until they've gotten several tattoos. At that point they may decide that they have the skills to become tattoo artists themselves.

The quality of a tattoo artist's work depends as much on his or her training than on any natural artistic talent. An aspiring tattooist should enter his or her apprenticeship with a basic knowledge of fundamental artistic concepts, such as perspective and shading. The tattooist needs to be able to translate a design from paper to skin, and even skilled artists can have trouble with making that jump.

Although the atmosphere inside a tattoo studio may be casual, a tattoo studio is still a place of work. When studios want to bring in new artists or apprentices, they look a candidate's employment history just as any other employer would. Hours may be flexible, but a tattoo artist needs to be dependable and show up on time for work shifts and appointments with customers.

The studio's owners may look into the artist's work history to see if he or she has a reputation for dependability and can make responsible decisions. Apprentices, especially those still in their teens, can highlight any summer or weekend jobs they've had, volunteer work, or leadership roles at school.

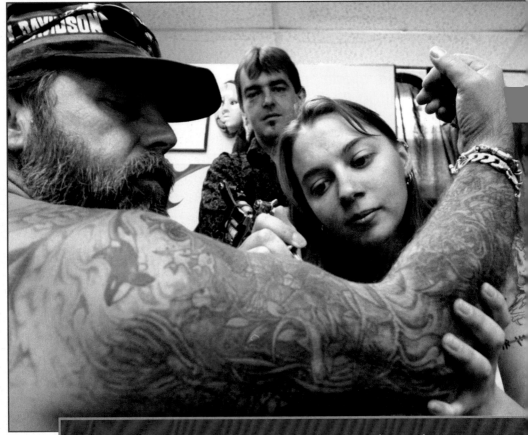

An apprentice tattooist adds to a customer's sleeve design while her mentor watches. Being given the chance to work on such a complex design is a sign of the tattoo artist's faith in her abilities.

Tattoo studio owners are aware of the reputation that businesses like theirs once had, so they may also look into the character of their artists. Some studios perform background checks on their artists to see if they're hiding criminal histories. The tattooing community can be very forgiving of a person's history, especially when any crimes committed happened a long time ago and were relatively minor in nature. However, they also want their artists to be open and honest about having any criminal record so that they

THE TATTOOED FELLOWSHIP

One of the most famous instances of friends using tattoos to show their bond came about after the cast of director Peter Jackson's *Lord of the Rings* movie trilogy finished filming. Eight of the nine actors who played central characters in the story decided to get tattoos to commemorate their work together. For the design, they chose to have the inscription be in Elvish, a language invented by author J. R. R. Tolkien, and translated as "nine." These stars, who included Ian McKellen, Elijah Wood, and Orlando Bloom, now carry with them a small piece of a film trilogy that touched many people.

are not surprised if this information comes out after they've been hired. Records of crimes committed by juveniles are generally kept sealed and off limits to background checks.

Studio owners may also want to make sure that alcohol and drug abuse are not problems for their artists. Drug testing for artists is not common among tattoo studios, but they still want the artists representing them to be sober and clearheaded when working. A botched tattoo by an artist under the influence of drugs or alcohol can destroy his or her reputation and harm that of the studio. A tattooist who makes a mistake like that would probably be fired.

Skills on Display

Most tattoo artists have portfolios, or collections of their best work. Tattoo portfolios often include photographs of tattoos that turned out extremely well, as well as designs and testimonials from happy customers. Beginning artists should have portfolios of artwork that they can show to studios as they seek apprenticeships. A beginner's portfolio can include examples of any type of art, but examples of drawings and paintings are more helpful than photography and sculpture. Examples of temporary tattoos created with paints or

A tattoo artist's portfolio should give customers a sense of his or her unique style, including elements such as the colors, characters, and shading he or she prefers to use.

henna can showcase an artist's ability to translate art skills to skin, as well as demonstrate the artist's dexterity and understanding of color.

A lot of thought should go into building a portfolio. A solid portfolio shows an artist's strengths and mastery of techniques. It should be carefully edited so that the artist's very best works are included. Some artists have a hard time sorting through their work and picking the best work, rather than their favorites. It may be helpful to have a teacher or a fellow artist help with selecting the best work for display.

Tattoo artists should work to add to their portfolio as they continue their careers. An art student's portfolio of paintings and drawings might help him or her get an apprenticeship at a shop. By the time the apprenticeship is finished, the apprentice artist should have a carefully selected portfolio of tattoo concepts and designs in a variety of styles.

CHAPTER Three

Learning the Trade

You probably don't need a college degree to become a tattoo artist, but you will likely need to serve an apprenticeship. Most states require some form of training and formal certification before an artist can go into business. The apprenticeship process gives people their first taste of what the business is like and covers what they need to know before they can start working.

Training to become a tattoo artist is unlike any other type of art education. For starters, a prospective tattooist should have a love of art and some level of artistic ability. He or she has to be willing and able to learn new artistic techniques and skills and then apply them in the studio. Unlike most other jobs in the arts, their creations will most likely remain a part of their customers' lives for many years to come. They take satisfaction in creating work that the customer can display with pride. Because their work involves modifying the bodies of their customers, tattoo artists have to learn how to do so safely. Learning all the artistic skills and tattooing laws and regulations as an apprentice can seem impossible. However, the lessons will sink in under the guidance of a good mentor.

A master tattoo artist discusses his designs with an apprentice. The willingness and ability to absorb lessons from a mentor is necessary for completing an apprenticeship.

Education Requirements

A person can become a tattoo artist without a college degree, but many states require tattooists to have at least a high school diploma or a graduate equivalency diploma (GED). There are no federal educational requirements for tattoo artists. Part of the licensing process for tattoo artists usually includes being tested on health and safety procedures, including preventing infection and the transmission of blood-borne diseases. Some first aid training and an understanding of biology and sanitary principles can be helpful in preparing for these classes.

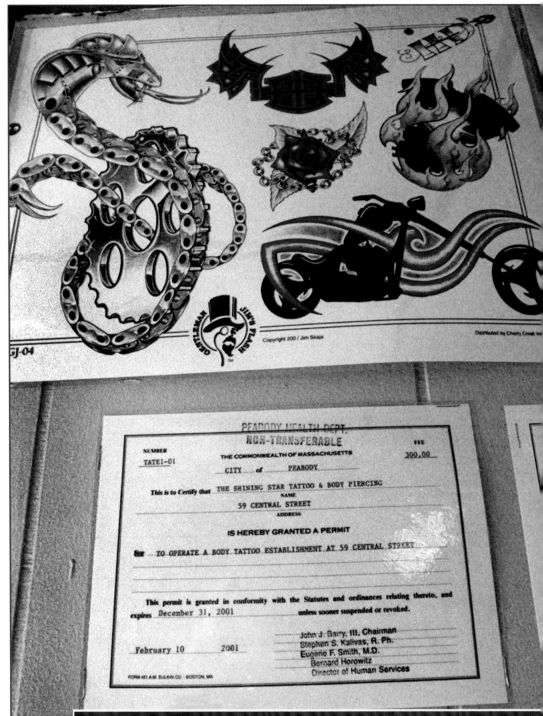

Most cities and towns require permits to operate tattoo studios. This tattoo establishment's permit is on display alongside some of the flash art that is available.

Basic first aid procedures are often required, including cardiopulmonary resuscitation (CPR). Artists have to receive CPR and first aid certification from a licensed instructor. Usually, this instruction includes hands-on training, such as performing CPR and practicing tourniquets and bandaging on dummies. Some state and local laws require tattoo artists to renew their certifications every few years, meaning that they have to take new classes or pass new tests. In some places, tattoo artists have to take classes and pass tests every year.

Most states require aspiring tattoo artists to serve apprenticeships under the guidance of experienced, licensed artists. Apprenticeship requirements differ from state to state, with the minimum length averaging from one to two years. The Alliance of Professional Tattooists recommends that apprenticeships last at least three years. In many cases, the apprenticeship does not end until the sponsoring artist says that the apprentice is ready. Apprenticeships with some artists can last several years.

Art classes or even artistic ability is not needed to complete the courses and pass the tests required by states to get a tattooing license. However, the apprentice's sponsor may want the aspiring tattooist to take classes to improve his or her art skills.

Finding a Sponsor

Many tattoo studios are willing to take on talented tattoo enthusiasts as apprentices, but it's important to choose the right artist to serve as a mentor. A particularly popular studio may have a long list of people who want to become apprentices. Larger studios

Apprentices, such as the woman pictured here, spend much of their time creating new designs. They may spend hours out of each day drawing and perfecting their art.

could have several apprentices, while smaller ones may have only one or two at a time, if any.

An aspiring tattooist may know who he or she wants to study under, but it can be hard to line up an apprenticeship with in-demand tattoo artists. The best way to get a chance at becoming an apprentice for such an artist is to get noticed. Develop a really strong portfolio of work and don't be shy about showing it around. Spend some time at the tattoo studio and get to know the artists. Talk to them about tattooing and show an interest in their work and the art that goes into their designs. Ask questions about how the shop is run, how a design is created, even about how the machines are cleaned. If you're old enough and have thought it through, consider getting tattooed by your favorite artist at the shop. After establishing a comfortable relationship with the shop and its artists, start letting them know that you are serious about wanting to become a tattoo artist. Offer to help out at the shop, perhaps by cleaning up or working at the reception desk. Above all, make sure that they see your portfolio and that it includes your very best work.

Be prepared for possible rejection. An artist may already have an apprentice and can't take on another. Some tattooists may not even take apprentices. An aspiring tattoo artist who gets turned down by the tattooist of his or her choice should accept the decision gracefully and look around for another mentor. If no one at your shop of choice can serve as a mentor, ask for a recommendation for someone at another shop. Most of all, look for an artist with several years of experience whom you think you will get along with over the course of three years.

Apprenticing costs money. Artists know that their skills and time are valuable, and very few offer apprenticeships for free. It will likely cost a few thousand dollars to complete an apprenticeship, though some artists charge less. Apprentices are almost never paid, so they usually need a job outside the tattoo shop or some other means of support. Artists can be flexible when scheduling their apprentices' shifts, so long as they show up when they are supposed to and are dedicated to doing a good job.

Most tattoo artists and studios are honest in their dealings with apprentices. Many set out terms of an apprenticeship in a contract, including how much they are supposed to work and what their responsibilities will be. A contract sets out the obligations of both parties and sets out terms for how they will be fulfilled. It protects both the artist and the apprentice by establishing boundaries and limits. In return, the artists offer one-on-one instruction on design creation and techniques. In return for work, they'll offer useful criticism and support.

Do your research before signing up for an apprenticeship with any shop. Talk to tattoo artists you respect to find out who trained them and whether they had good or bad experiences. Do searches for news stories or public records that might point to a history of fraud or criminal activity at a studio. Avoid seeking internships at such places. Learning from an artist with a bad reputation in the tattooing community can hurt an apprentice's chances of becoming an artist at another studio.

Tattooing isn't typically offered as a course of study at vocational schools, community colleges, or other traditional job training institutions. There are some places that set themselves up as "tattoo schools" where aspiring artists can learn about tattooing and get certified without going through an apprenticeship.

Tattooing schools are controversial in the tattooing world. Artists often criticize them for teaching what they see as an assembly line approach to tattooing that stifles creativity. To them, these schools flood the market with artists who do not have the proper skills to create a good tattoo. The programs can be pricey and don't offer the same level of personal support and interaction as a traditional apprenticeship. Tattoo schools counter that they provide a solid education in tattoo basics in a safe and sterile environment. Their programs take less time to complete, usually one to two years, whereas tattoo artists may keep apprentices working for them for much longer. For the most part, people in the tattooing community prefer artists who trained with other artists to those who learned in a tattoo school program.

Developing a Style

Apprentices usually start their training with an idea of what their style will be. They may already have tattoos in a certain style that they like or an artist whose work they admire and wish to emulate. They may have work in their preferred style in their portfolio, or

Tattootists—such as the one shown here working on a customer's tattoo—may themselves have body work done in their preferred style.

they may just have an idea of what kind of work they want to do. Having a style in mind before beginning an apprenticeship is always a positive step. However, be prepared to see that style change as the apprenticeship continues. Apprentices are expected to learn many different styles, and it's possible that you will find another style you like. Also keep in mind that some styles may be very difficult to apply to tattooing and that you may have to adapt yours or find a new style.

If possible, it is best to apprentice under an artist whose work you appreciate. Watch the artist as closely as you can while he or she works (if the customer doesn't mind) to get an idea of how artistic techniques are applied during the process. Ask questions when possible and pay attention to each part of the process. Some of the most important work the artist does actually comes before he or she starts using the tattoo machine.

Ending the Apprenticeship

There's no set time for how long an apprenticeship lasts. Typically, an apprentice isn't ready to become a full-fledged tattoo artist until his or her mentor decides he or she is ready. A contract between the apprentice and the mentor might set an ending time for the apprenticeship, but the length of that agreement depends on how long the artist wants to train the apprentice. There is no average time, but apprentices can generally count on spending at least two to three years learning the craft.

Some contracts might be set up so that the apprenticeship is complete once the apprentice

SEEKING AN APPRENTICESHIP

It can take many years of practice and patience before an aspiring tattooist manages to get an apprenticeship. Pioneering tattoo artist Vyvyn Lazonga had a hard time finding an artist who would mentor her during the early 1970s. Writing for the website Tattoo Road Trip, she offers the following advice to people seeking an apprenticeship:

- *Get tattooed before approaching anyone.*
- *Draw all the time.*
- *Don't ask for an apprenticeship. Instead, make yourself useful around the shop.*
- *Expect to work hard for zero wages.*
- *Have a humble attitude.*
- *Don't walk into a shop without knowing any-thing about it beforehand.*
- *Don't think you can teach yourself all the skills you need to become an artist.*
- *Respect yourself and the art.*

achieves certain milestones, such as a set number of hours of observing tattoos being applied or mastering a certain number of styles. The mentor might require the apprentice to pass certain health or art classes before declaring the apprentice ready. It's even pos-sible that the mentor decides that the apprentice will never master the skills necessary to become a tattoo artist and ends the agreement early. In such cases, the artist may refund some of the money the apprentice paid to be trained. The apprentice can then look for another artist who is willing to serve as a mentor or consider another line of work.

The end of a successful apprenticeship is usually a time of triumph. After years of hard work, the apprentice's skills as an artist are finally validated. The mentor presents the apprentice with a certificate, which serves as proof to regulators that he or she met the apprenticeship requirement. Once the apprenticeship is complete, the former apprentice can focus on the process of getting a license and then on getting a job. After working so closely under one mentor for such a long time, it's not unusual for an apprentice to develop a very strong bond with the artists in that shop and with the customers. He or she may be offered a job there once the licensing process is complete or at the very least will likely get good references from the experience.

CHAPTER Four

Licensing and Standards

States regulate how tattoo studios operate, from the licensing process to health standards. Each state has different regulations and requirements related to how licenses are issued and what a person needs to do to be licensed. Most states require artists to be at least eighteen years old and to have completed an apprenticeship. Artists will likely be a few years older by the time they get licensed, as most shops won't accept apprentices younger than age eighteen. Prospective tattoo artists also have to meet health and safety standards and prove that they can master first aid and disease prevention techniques.

Protecting Health and Safety

The health and safety standards that tattoo artists must meet are geared toward preventing diseases from spreading and protecting customers from developing infections. Standards differ from state to state. An artist who is looking to move to another state or who works in different states will have to make sure that he or she meets the necessary requirements and is fully licensed to work at each location.

There are rules governing how tattoo studios go about many aspects of their work. Although the

Tattoo machines and ink sit prepped and ready on a sterile surface. Sterilization in an autoclave helps prevent the spread of disease and is usually required by law.

particulars of licensing and operating requirements may be slightly different from state to state, there are some rules that are fairly universal. Rules state how many sinks a tattoo parlor can have, what kind of wall covering, floor, and even ceiling can be in a tattooing workstation, and even the type of cleaning products that can be used. State laws specify how tattooing tools are treated. They usually have to be scrubbed and then sterilized in an auto-clave, and new instruments must be kept separate from those that have been used. Artists are required to wear sterile latex gloves and may also be required to wear aprons and face masks. Even if those extra steps are not required, some artists wear them anyway, both for their own safety and for the safety of their customers.

When it comes to applying the tattoo, there are more rules that the artist has to follow. The law usually requires that people sign

Some states allow teenagers to get tattoos if the teen has permission from a parent. However, it is usually up to the tattoo artist to decide whether he or she will work on young customers.

a form stating that they understand the risks of getting a tattoo, such as the possibility of an allergic reaction to pigments in the ink or of unwanted scar tissue, that they are legally old enough, and that they give their consent to have the procedure carried out.

In most states, the customer will have to prove that he or she is legally old enough to get a tattoo or have permission from a parent or guardian. Thirty-eight states have laws requiring permission from a parent or guardian, and some require the person granting permission to be present. In some states, such as New York, Illinois, Maine, and Alaska, it is illegal to tattoo a minor even with parental permission. Some states, such as Pennsylvania and Indiana, require that the parent or guardian be present while the minor is tattooed, while others require only written consent. In Nevada, it is illegal for a person younger than eighteen even to loiter in a tattooing area. Nonetheless, in states where it is legal to tattoo minors without the consent of their parents, tattoo studios and individual artists have the right to refuse.

Many shops won't tattoo someone who is obviously ill or intoxicated. Tattooing a sick person can make the tattoo artist ill and can contaminate a studio. A person who is drunk or high might have a bad physical reaction to being tattooed. For example, alcohol thins the blood and can cause a person to bleed heavily, which can be dangerous if he or she is getting tattooed. In addition, intoxicated people may not be considered capable of understanding a consent form, even if they sign one. Even in places where it is legal to get a tattoo while intoxicated, many studios refuse to serve these clients because of the risks involved.

ARTIST PROFILE: JORDAN MITCHELL

Jordan Mitchell is a tattoo artist and illustrator at Black and Blue Tattoo in San Francisco, California. In an interview with the graphic art online marketplace 99designs.com, he said he first became interested in tattoos when he was a teen. He loved to draw and study comic books, and when he turned eighteen years old, he became an apprentice tattoo artist at his friend's father's studio in Modesto, California. Mitchell said that he first decided on a career in the arts because he loved drawing so much, and he was inspired to study tattooing by the high-quality body art he saw in tattooing magazines.

Mitchell didn't start with a formal arts background, but he later realized how much it could help him develop as an artist. When he reached a lull in his tattooing career, he decided to take college classes to take his art to the next level. Mitchell studied art fundamentals and took classes in observational skills and figure drawing. Today, he encourages tattoo artists to try new things to find inspiration for their work and to keep learning.

Art students practice figure drawing techniques before an exam. Taking classes in the fine arts can give tattooists new ideas and help them refine their designs.

Preventing Diseases

Most states require tattoo artists to take classes and pass tests on disease prevention before they can be licensed. The specific requirements might differ a little from state to state, but for the most part tattoo artists are expected to know about diseases that are transmitted through blood—such as HIV, hepatitis, and tuberculosis—and standards for preventing their spread. In Oklahoma, for example, tattooists have to show proof that they have completed training in blood-borne pathogens and that they have CPR certification. Florida requires tattoo artists to take and pass a three-hour course on blood-borne pathogens such as bacteria and

An allergy to tattoo ink caused this person's rash, which can be treated with lotions or prescription drugs. More serious conditions such as HIV and hepatitis can be spread through tattooing equipment that has not been properly cleaned.

fungi and communicable diseases. Other states have similar licensing requirements. Check with the state health department to find out what the licensing requirements are in your area.

Preventing diseases and infections is a priority for tattoo artists. Most tattooists wear sterile disposable gloves when working. Some wear masks and aprons. Sinks are usually required for each tattooing area. Surfaces typically have to be wipeable, meaning that they must be smooth, nonabsorbent, and easy to clean, with no space for bacteria to hide.

Autoclaves, which are machines that use steam heat and pressure to sterilize items such as instruments and clothing, are standard equipment for most tattoo studios and are usually required by law. To be

A regional environmental health specialist is reflected in the door of an autoclave while she reviews safety procedures at a tattoo shop in San Diego, California.

effective against all blood-borne pathogens, an auto-clave has to be capable of reaching temperatures of at least 246 degrees Fahrenheit (119 degrees Celsius) and maintain those temperatures for at least thirty minutes. Autoclaves should be inspected regularly to make sure they are working properly.

Towels and other linens, instruments, and other small equipment can be sterilized in an autoclave. Furnishings such as the chairs that people sit in while they are tattooed, lamps and magnifiers the artists use, sinks, counters, and trays are sterilized with chemical disinfectants. Although some parts of the tattoo machine are small enough to clean in an autoclave, others are bulky and have to be dis-infected. Cleanliness is also usually required in the lobby and other public places.

Regulating Business

Tattoo studios are highly regulated because of the health risks involved with the business. State and local governments usually have the authority to inspect businesses to make sure that conditions inside are safe and don't pose a threat. In a city, there may be separate inspections to make sure the structure is sound, there's no danger of fire, and that wiring and plumbing codes are being fol-lowed. Workplace safety inspectors may come in to make sure that working conditions are safe for employees. For tattoo studios, health inspectors are usually the most important of these visitors. They make sure that the studio and its artists are following any safety standards required by state and local law. Bad reports from a health inspector can force a tattoo studio to shut down if the problems aren't fixed and can lead to artists losing their licenses.

Other regulations have to do with where and when tattoo shops can open. Towns have zoning laws that state where certain kinds of businesses can be located. A town's zoning laws may not allow tattoo studios to be located in the main downtown area or within a certain distance of schools or homes. Sometimes a tattoo artist can get a special permit to open in one of these restricted areas if he or she works closely with the town and the community to show that the studio poses no threat to that community. Regulations also may govern how late the tattoo shop can open. For example, it may be illegal to keep the studio open past a certain hour as a way to discourage intoxicated people from getting tattoos.

State and local inspectors check to make sure studios are following the law. Concerned citizens may also report any unauthorized or illegal activity at a studio. However, a tattooist should not obey the law out of fear of getting caught doing something illegal. Just like other businesses on the block, he or she should follow the rules to be a good neighbor. Maintaining a good relationship with other businesses and with the town government helps encourage people to come to the studio. It usually becomes known that the owner is honest, trustworthy, and follows the rules to protect his or her customers and community.

CHAPTER *Five*

The Artist's Life

Unless they own their own shops, tattoo artists are usually contract employees who share studio space and equipment with other artists. Some stay in the same studio for many years; others may switch studios every few years because they want a change of pace. They usually don't draw a salary from their studios. Instead they are paid by their customers and in turn often pay a portion of their earnings to the studio's owner in exchange for use of the space and equipment.

Artists also enjoy a great deal of freedom in what they do. Their designs are their own, and their reputation is built on the quality of their work. Tattooing is a skill that artists can take anywhere and a profession that they can practice in any state, provided they can get a license. They're in the business because they love tattooing and they're passionate about creating quality art.

Getting Paid

Being a tattoo artist has some challenges. Most artists are not paid by the studios where they work and likely have to pay rent to the studio owners. Instead,

Flash tattoo designs like the ones shown here are often easy for artists to do. They can be finished quickly, and many tattooists charge flat fees for them rather than an hourly rate.

they are paid directly by their customers. They usually have to pay for their own health insurance and probably don't have retirement benefits or even paid time off. Studios may take a small percentage out of each payment for expenses. During busy periods, this might not be a problem. Summer vacation is usually a time when people choose to get tattoos. In college towns and cities with big universities, the beginning of the school year can bring in a lot of business as students new to the area look to get tattooed.

However, tattoo artists often face slow times, such as when the economy is bad and people don't have the extra money to spend on tattoos. Winter months can also be slow, as people aren't as interested in displaying body art when the weather is cold. Some tattoo artists may even spend slow months working in other cities where demand is higher throughout the year. Others may have second jobs, either in the arts or in an entirely different field.

The U.S. Department of Labor does not provide detailed information regarding pay and benefits for tattoo artists, though there are some recent surveys that offer an idea of how much a tattooist can make. Check out online sources such as the job search firm SimplyHired.com and the Wisconsin Department of Workforce Development (dwd.wisonsin.gov) or other similar websites to investigate average earning ranges. Senior tattoo artists with many years of experience may set hourly rates that they charge customers. The rate may be adjusted depending on the size and the complexity of the design, as well as its placement and how long the artist estimates the work will take to finish. Hourly rates are most commonly set for custom designs, particularly those on which the artist and the customer have worked together. Tattoo artists with less experience may not give hourly rates, mostly because they usually take longer to complete jobs and trying to work faster would risk botching the tattoo. Hourly rates are usually more than $100, and some of the best-known and most skilled artists can command rates of several hundred dollars per hour.

Artists who charge flat rates may take several factors into account when setting their fees. Custom

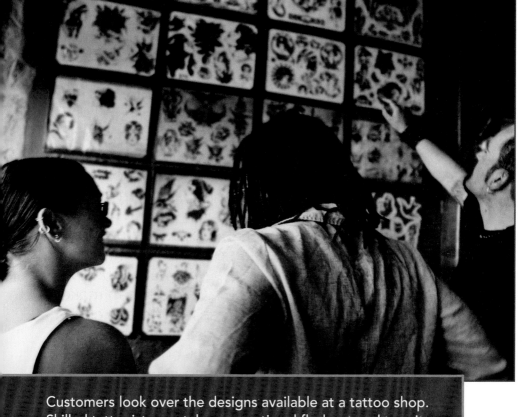

Customers look over the designs available at a tattoo shop. Skilled tattooists can take conventional flash art and turn it into something special or use it to help a client create a custom image.

work is usually more expansive than a "flash" tattoo. Flash tattoos are usually generic tattoo designs that are on display to give customers ideas for body art. They also serve as templates for walk-in customers who want quick tattoos and don't have any interest in custom work. These designs are usually less expensive because they are very familiar to a tattoo artist and take less time to complete. Beginning artists may work exclusively with flash tattoos while the shop's more experienced tattooists do the custom work.

Tools of the Trade

Once a tattoo artist is certified and has found a place in a studio, he or she needs to have the necessary tools to work in the field. Some equipment is provided by the tattoo studio and are for the use of all the artists who work there. Other items have to be bought by the artists themselves.

Tattoo machines are the core of any tattoo artist's equipment. Just as in prehistoric days, artists use needles to embed ink beneath the customer's skin. In the past, this work was done pinprick by pinprick, using a needle or some similar sharp object. Hundreds or even thousands of such pinpricks are needed to complete most tattoos. As the needle pierces the skin, the coloring agent is injected or rubbed into it. Although some artists today will use traditional methods to create tattoos, most tattooists use electric tattoo machines that can make hundreds of pinpricks per minute. They vary in power and complexity.

All electric tattoo machines run off of direct current electricity (most household appliances are powered by alternating current) and they need power adapters before they can be plugged into wall sockets. Settings allow the artist to control the speed and precision of the machine.

Tattoo machines are made to move tattoo needles, which insert ink beneath the skin. More than one needle is usually working at once, cutting the time it takes to get a tattoo. Needles can be arranged in certain patterns to accomplish particular tasks, such as shading a large area or completing a bit of fine detail. Artists usually experiment with needle arrangements before figuring out what works best for them.

The inks used in tattooing are specially formulated from pigment powders suspended in a liquid consisting of water and either alcohol, glycerin, or propylene glycol (sometimes called a carrier). Pigments are made from any number of materials, including carbon and metals. Artists can buy inks premixed or mix their own.

Other equipment and supplies are far less specialized. Razors are used to shave the area where the tattoo will be applied. The artist cleans the area thoroughly with antibacterial soap. An artist uses transfer paper and pencils to outline a tattoo on a customer's skin before getting to work with the tattoo machine. When the tattoo is finished, cotton swabs will be used to absorb any blood, and a gauze covering will be taped over the fresh tattoo.

Sterile gloves are always worn when handling tattoo machines. Here, an artist is shown assembling her tattoo machine before beginning a design.

Making Lasting Work

A tattoo is intended to last forever, and tattoo artists know that people will carry their work on their bodies for years to come. This aspect drives most artists to be the very best that they can be. Still, the gap separating the best tattoo artist from the worst is incredibly large. Many of the best artists have such large followings that they have become their own brands. Celebrities go to them

THE HAND TAPPING RENAISSANCE

Most tattooists today use a tattoo machine to create their images. However, a small and growing number of artists are reviving the practice of hand tapping tattoos—using traditional methods to apply tattoos. Advocates of hand-tapping techniques, which involve making each needle mark individually, use a needle attached to a wooden stick. The artist uses another stick to gently tap it until the needle is inserted in the skin and the dye is embedded. Instead of relying on the tattoo machine's settings, an artist has to use his or her sense of touch to determine when the needle is deep enough into the skin. The process is far more time-consuming than using a machine, but some artists prefer to tattoo by feel. Some customers also prefer hand-tapped tattoos over the buzz and constant pressure of a tattoo machine.

for body art, and some have become prominent outside the world of tattooing.

For most artists, tattooing can be an up and down business. They go through times when they are very busy, followed by stretches in which they don't have many customers. These can be difficult times for tattoo artists, but they can also opportunities to sharpen skills. Artists can use their free time to work on new designs and try different styles.

Before work on a tattoo begins, the artist sits down with the customer to talk about the design and placement. The conversation may be a long one if the client has very specific ideas about what he or she wants. For custom work, the customer might make a separate appointment just to talk about the design. The artist will offer any input on the design and they will talk about elements such as color, shading, and where the tattoo will be placed on the body. The artist will do a sketch to show the customer how it will look, even if the customer has brought in his or her own image.

Once the artist and the customer agree on how the image will look, they talk about where to put it. The customer gets final say over where a tattoo will go, but the artist will offer input if the customer wants an image in a particularly difficult place to tattoo or in a spot where there won't be enough room to ink the image. The artist may even decide that he or she can't do the tattoo because of the placement, in which case he or she may recommend another artist or simply and politely thank the customer and end the appointment. Learning how to handle such negotiations firmly and politely is a big part of being a successful tattoo artist. Still, always remember that the customer has the final say in how a tattoo will look. Making the customer happy and providing a safe, friendly atmosphere can help generate good public relations and bring in more clients.

Most important, keep practicing. If there's a lull in action at the studio, spend the time drawing. Sketch during your spare time, whether it's first thing in the morning, during lunch, or while you are commuting. Show your drawings to the tattoo artists at your studio and get their advice on your work. Continue to practice new styles to hone your skills.

Removing Tattoos

Tattoo removal is a controversial subject among tattoo artists. Some won't even cover up another artist's work with a tattoo of their own design. However, a growing number of studios are recognizing that some customers have tattoos that have become damaged or that they no longer like and now offer removal services. Most tattoo removal is done using lasers, which blast the tattooed area with an intense beam of light. The process is painful—many removal customers compare it to being burned with hot wax—and can take several sessions, depending on the size of the image and the color of the ink used to create it. Even then, a partial image or a mark may still be visable where the tattoo once was.

The lasers used in tattoo removal are powerful tools, and special certifications are needed before they can be used. The certification standards vary from state to state. Typically, an artist can earn his or her laser removal certification by taking a class, which may be offered at a community college or technical

A nurse practitioner at a tattoo removal clinic in California uses a laser to erase a tattoo from a man's neck. This clinic offers free removal services for some body art.

institute. Most states consider tattoo removal to be a medical procedure, but only six require that a doctor be present.

Knowing Your Clientele

Tattoo artists work with all kinds of people. Some customers may be happy to come in and get one tattoo without ever really thinking about getting another. Others may be tattoo enthusiasts who regularly add to their body art. Getting to know the local tattoo community and what the clientele likes helps an artist to get established. Some local themes may come up regularly in body art, such as sports team insignia or fraternity and sorority symbols. Get involved with the community and local interests so that you can find common ground with customers. Even small tattoos take a while to create, and the time passes faster for the customer if the artist can maintain a conversation and shows an interest in people who frequent the studio.

CHAPTER *Six*

Opening for Business

Striking out on your own takes courage, and many tattoo artists never make the leap to opening their own studios. Opening a studio is expensive and involves a lot of work with no guarantee of success, but for some artists, it's worth the risk.

The decision to open any small business should not be taken lightly. An artist who wants to open his or her own studio should have enough money saved to pay expenses such as rent, utility bills, and salaries for at least several months, as well as any licensing fees and insurance costs. Unless the artist is taking over another tattoo studio, he or she will probably have to do some renovations inside so that the studio meets code requirements. Considering these expenses, it may take the new studio some time to attract customers and start making money. Artists may want to look into small business loans or contemplate taking on partners to help cover expenses until the business becomes profitable.

It is best to start out with a solid business plan that anticipates expenses and predicts income.

Decide early on whether or not to take on a partner or two so that the relationship is well established when the shop opens. Also decide how many artists to bring in at the beginning and whether or not to offer additional body art services, such as piercing. Contact these artists early on and get them to commit to working in your studio, preferably by signing a contract. With luck, they will bring their own customer base with them when they start working in your studio.

Finding a Space

Choosing a location is one of the most basic steps in opening a tattoo studio. Pick a place that is convenient to the clientele you want to serve. If the studio is going to serve a large area and won't have much local competition, opening along a busy street or road with plenty of parking available might be a good option. If you want to open in a downtown area, try choosing a location near a major attraction that brings in a lot of foot traffic. Opening near businesses that keep late hours can help bring in customers throughout the day and into the evening. Above all, look for a place where the studio will be convenient to get to and easy to find, yet still affordable to rent. It may be wise to set a limit on how much you're willing to pay for rent each month before looking for locations.

Zoning regulations may play a role in where to locate a studio. Check to make sure your city's or town's zoning code allows tattoo studios at a particular location before signing a lease agreement. Take a close look at the building itself to see how much remodeling will be needed before a studio can open.

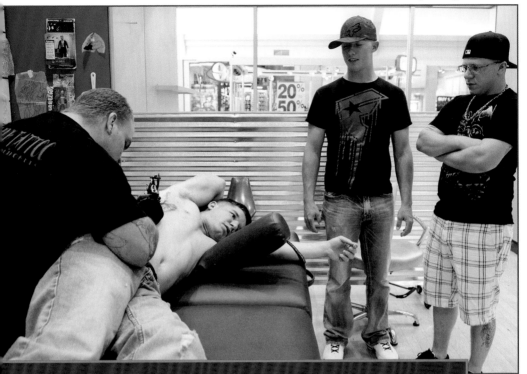

Two marines watch as their comrade gets a tattoo on his rib cage at a studio that is located in a shopping mall. Tattoos can be a way for people who have shared experiences to show their bond.

An attractive space may turn out to be more expensive than it is worth if it requires major remodeling work. Be sure to talk to other local business owners about a site's history and whether an area would be welcoming to a tattoo studio.

Hiring Staff

Finding the right people to work in a tattoo studio can be a time-consuming process. Choose artists who do good work, are reliable, and are not afraid to take a chance on a new studio. Artists may be reluctant to leave a studio where they have an

TATTOO EXPOS EXPOSED

Anyone wanting an inside look at the world of tattooing should consider going to a tattoo expo or convention. The Hell City Tattoo Festival, held each year in Phoenix, Arizona, and in Columbus, Ohio, is one of the largest such events. New York City boasts several tattoo expos, including the New York City Tattoo Convention and the New York Empire State Tattoo Expo. Expos are large, often regional gatherings of body art professionals and enthusiasts. Tattoo artists (and often body piercers) set up booths to

A man relaxes while getting tattooed at a body art expo held in California. These events give tattoo artists a chance to meet one another and have their work exposed to new potential clients.

show off their portfolios, take part in panel discussions, mingle with each other, and sometimes even create tattoos. These events are also places where artists can take necessary health and safety classes. Some expos offer artists the chance to enter competitions in which a panel of judges rate the quality of an artist's work. For artists, expos offer a rare opportunity to meet with other tattooists and learn about what is new in the industry.

established clientele and a comfortable relationship with their fellow artists.

Finding skilled, responsible workers may take time. Some tattooists open new studios without bringing in another artist. They may have only an administrative assistant to help out with scheduling and tasks such as cleaning or a part-time accountant to take care of the studio's finances. Bringing in an apprentice can help relieve the workload, while providing the extra benefit of training someone who might be willing to work in the shop once he or she becomes licensed. However, bringing in other licensed tattoo artists or body piercers can help cover expenses and bring more customers to the shop.

Building a Clientele

Tattoo artists usually attract new customers through word of mouth. People who want to get a tattoo often ask their tattooed friends where they had their body art done and whether they recommend those artists. Tattoo enthusiasts often share the positive—and negative—experiences they've had at particular

Tattooists display some of the designs they've created during an international tattoo convention held in Quito, Ecuador. Such gatherings can help an artist develop a following across several countries.

studios. This word of mouth advertising can easily make or break a studio that has just opened. Online review sites such as Yelp and message boards have made it even easier for tattoo enthusiasts to share their experiences with one another and recommend artists.

Tattooists also build their clientele through traditional means, such as media advertising and promotions. Signs and ads in newspapers, in magazines, and on websites can attract new clients who are curious about a recently opened shop. Promotional efforts such as discounts and coupons can also help bring in people who might turn into regular customers. For example, tattoo shops in college towns may offer a student discount to anyone who shows a valid college ID. Attending conventions and expos can also help bring in more business.

Ultimately, the most important promotional work is done in the shop and in the neighborhood. Providing quality tattoos in a safe environment and at a fair price is the best way to get regulars to come back to the shop and recommend it to their friends. Providing a welcoming atmosphere where people can come into the studio to look at designs and talk to artists can put prospective customers at ease and encourage them to get tattoos there. Getting involved with the community by joining local business organizations, doing volunteer work, and sponsoring events can help publicize a shop and bring in new clients. Through hard work and being a good neighbor, a tattoo artist can become an important and respected part of the community.

GLOSSARY

ADJACENT Near or next to something else.

ANTIBACTERIAL Able to destroy bacteria or hinder their growth.

APPRENTICE Someone who works for a particular person or company, often for little or no pay, to learn a profession.

AUTOCLAVE A device used for heating objects beyond the boiling point to make them sterile.

COLLABORATION The process of working with someone to produce something.

CONTAMINATION The process of making something dirty, polluted, or poisonous by adding a chemical, waste, or infection.

CUSTOM Made according to the instructions or specifications of an individual.

DIVERSIFICATION The process of developing new skills or expanding offerings.

EMPHASIS Special attention or importance that is given to one thing in particular.

FLASH Pictures of tattoos and designs that are already available and don't require customization.

HEPATITIS An infectious inflammation of the liver caused by a virus or toxin.

HIV Human immunodeficiency virus; the virus that causes AIDS.

INFECTION A disease or other medical condition caused by bacteria, a virus, or a parasite.

MAINSTREAM Considered usual and ordinary by most people.

MENTOR An experienced person who helps someone who has much less experience.

PIGMENT A natural substance that gives color to something, such as dye or paint.

PLACEMENT The act of putting something in a certain position or location.

PORTFOLIO A collection of examples of an artist's work, often kept in a folder, a book, or within digital folders.

REPERTOIRE The full range of things that someone in a particular field can do.

REPUTATION A common opinion held by many about someone or something.

STERILE Clean and free of bacteria and other contaminants that could cause an infection.

FOR MORE INFORMATION

Alliance of Professional Tattooists
215 West 18th Street, Suite 210
Kansas City, MO 64108
(816) 979-1300
Website: http://www.safe-tattoos.com
This alliance provides information about tattoo safety and professional standards and guidelines for artists.

Baltimore Tattoo Museum
1534 Eastern Avenue
Baltimore, MD 21231
(410) 522-5800
Website: http://www.baltimoretattoomuseum.net
This museum features exhibits on the history of tattooing and also serves as a fully-functioning tattoo shop.

National Tattoo Association
485 Business Park Lane
Allentown, PA 18109-9120
(610) 433-7261
Website: http://www.nationaltattooassociation.com
This association is dedicated to the advancement of quality, safety standards, and professionalism in the tattoo community.

Public Health Agency of Canada
130 Colonnade Road
A.L. 6501H
Ottawa, ON K1A 0K9
Canada
(613) 957-2991

Website: http://www.phac-aspc.gc.ca
The agency offers information on public health topics, including tattooing and blood-borne diseases such as hepatitis.

Tattoo Art
Website: http://www.tattooartists.org
This online forum offers image galleries, message boards, and a marketplace for tattoo artists.

Worldwide Tattoo Canada
Unit C-7167 Gilley Avenue
Burnaby, BC V5J 4W9
Canada
(604) 438-9700
Website: http://www.worldwidetattoo.ca/english
Worldwide Tattoo manufactures and sells tattooing materials and equipment.

Websites

Because of the changing nature of Internet links, Rosen Publishing has developed an online list of websites related to the subject of this book. This site is updated regularly. Please use this link to access the list:

http://www.rosenlinks.com/CIYC/Tat

FOR FURTHER READING

Alayon, Erick. *The Complete Art of Tattooing.* CreateSpace Independent Publishing, 2012.

Bánfalvi, Ákos. *The Modern Masters of Tattooing: Exclusive Interviews with a Few of the Best Tattoo Artists of the New Generation from Around the World.* Atglen, PA: Schiffer Publishing, 2014.

Bergamotto, Lori. *Skin: The Bare Facts.* San Francisco, CA: Zest Books, 2010.

Christen, Carol, and Richard N. Bolles. *What Color Is Your Parachute? For Teens.* Emeryville, CA: Ten Speed Press, 2010.

Cohen, Robert. *Body Piercing and Tattooing* (Making Smart Choices). New York, NY: Rosen Publishing, 2013.

Deter-Wolf, Aaron, and Carol Diaz-Granados, eds. *Drawing with Great Needles: Ancient Tattoo Traditions of North America.* Austin, TX: University of Texas Press, 2013.

Fitzgerald, Isaac, and Wendy MacNaughton. *Pen & Ink: Tattoos and the Stories Behind Them.* New York, NY: Bloomsbury USA, 2014.

Gerber, Larry. *Getting Inked: What to Expect When You Get a Tattoo.* New York, NY: Rosen Publishing, 2012.

Gordon, Stephen G. *Expressing the Inner Wild: Tattoos, Piercings, Jewelry, and Other Body Art.* Minneapolis, MN: Lerner Publishing, 2014.

Hall, Gregory. *Tattoos: Should I or Shouldn't I?* Cleveland, OH: Gregory Hall, MD, 2011.

Hardy, Lal. *The Mammoth Book of Tattoos.* Philadelpia, PA: Running Press, 2009.

Hemingson, Vince. *Tattoo Design Directory.* Surrey, England: Chartwell Books, 2009.

Irish, Lora. *Great Book of Tattoo Designs, Rev. ed.: More Than 500 Body Art Designs.* East Petersburg, PA: Fox Chapel Publishing, 2013.

Kaplan, Michael B. *Tattoo World.* New York, NY: Abrams, 2011.

LaCour, Nina. *The Disenchantments.* New York, NY: Speak, 2013.

Lanser, Amanda. *Otzi the Iceman* (Digging Up the Past). Minneapolis, MN: Essential Library, 2014.

Schaller, Rhonda. *Create Your Art Career.* New York, NY: Skyhorse Publishing, 2013.

Spilsbury, Richard. *I'm Good at Art: What Job Can I Get?* London, England: Wayland, 2014.

Stewart, Gail. *A Cultural History of Tattoos.* San Diego, CA: ReferencePoint Press, 2013.

Von D, Kat. *High Voltage Tattoo.* New York, NY: HarperCollins, 2009.

Waterhouse, Jo. *Art by Tattooists: Beyond Flash.* London, England: Pinter & Martin, 2012.

BIBLIOGRAPHY

Andreatta, David. "Are Tattoo Studios 'Artists' Studios? Pittsford Says No." *Democrat & Chronicle*, October 23, 2014. Retrieved October 29, 2014 (http://www.democratandchronicle.com/story/news/2014/10/23/tattoo-studios-artists-studios-pittsford-says/17791449/).

Chambers, Jesse. "How Much Does Laser Tattoo Removal Cost? Answers to Questions About the Painful but Popular Procedure." AL.com, October 23, 2014. Retrieved November 23, 2014 (http://www.al.com/living/index.ssf/2014/11/post_201.html).

Flaming Gun Tattoo Studio. "Apprenticeship." Retrieved November 10, 2014 (http://www.flamingguntattoo.com/Apprenticeship.htm).

Goodman, Eleanor. "How to Be a Tattooist." *Bizarre*, May 2010. Retrieved October 15, 2014 (http://www.bizarremag.com/tattoos-and-bodyart/tattoos/9409/how_to_be_a_tattooist.html).

Harris Polls. "One in Five U.S. Adults Now Has a Tattoo." Harris Interactive, February 23, 2012. Retrieved September 8, 2014 (http://www.harrisinteractive.com/NewsRoom/HarrisPolls/tabid/447/mid/1508/articleId/970/ctl/ReadCustom%20Default/Default.aspx).

Ilasco, Meg Mateo, and Joy Deangdeelert Cho. *Creative, Inc.: The Ultimate Guide to Running a Successful Freelance Business.* San Francisco, CA: Chronicle Books, 2010.

Johnson, Jeff A. *Tattoo Machine: Tall Tales, True Stories, and My Life in Ink.* New York, NY: Spiegel & Grau, 2009.

Lazonga, Vyvyn. "For People Seeking to Become a Tattoo Artist." Tattoo Road Trip, May 4, 2011. Retrieved

November 12, 2014 (http://tattooroadtrip.com/for
-people-seeking-to-become-a-tattoo-artist).

Matchan, Linda. "As Laser Tattoo Removal Expands,
So Do Questions." *The Boston Globe*, May 31,
2013. Retrieved November 23, 2014 (http://www
.bostonglobe.com/lifestyle/style/2013/05/30
/laser-tattoo-removal-studios-are-increase
/2jqxGGopt11MIPdM4xaqiK/story.html).

Mayo Clinic Staff. "Tattoos: Understanding Risks and
Precautions." Retrieved October 10, 2014 (http://
www.mayoclinic.org/healthy-living/adult-health
/in-depth/tattoos-and-piercings/art-20045067).

Miller, Jean-Chris. *The Body Art Book.* New York, NY:
Berkley Books, 1997.

National Conference of State Legislatures. "Tattoos
and Body Piercings for Minors." May 2013.
Retrieved November 5, 2014 (http://www.ncsl
.org/research/health/tattooing-and-body
-piercing.aspx).

Occupational Safety and Health Administration.
"Bloodborne Pathogens and Needlestick Prevention." Retrieved October 6, 2014 (https://www
.osha.gov/SLTC/bloodbornepathogens).

Sanders, Clinton, and D. Angus Vail. *Customizing the
Body: The Art and Culture of Tattooing.* Philadel-
phia, PA: Temple University Press, 2008.

Surless, Joy. *Tattoo: From Idea to Ink.* Stillwater, MN:
Wolfgang Publications, 2008.

The Tattoo Collection. "Choosing a Tattoo Artist."
Retrieved October 17, 2014 (http://www
.thetattoocollection.com/choosing_a_tattoo
_artist.htm).

Thai, Stephanie. "An Interview with Tattoo Artist and
Illustrator Jordan Mitchell." 99Designs, September

23, 2014. Retrieved November 3, 2014 (http://99designs.com/designer-blog/2014/09/08/design-spotlight-jordan-mitchell-tattoo-artist).

Thobo-Carlsen, Mik. "How Tattoos Went from Subculture to Pop Culture." Huffington Post, October 27, 2014. Retrieved November 5, 2014 (http://www.huffingtonpost.com/mik-thobocarlsen/how-tattoos-went-from-sub_b_6053588.html).

Thompson, Scott. "What Makes a Tattoo Artist a Professional?" *Houston Chronicle*. Retrieved November 3, 2014 (http://work.chron.com/tattoo-artist-professional-18896.html).

U.S. Food and Drug Administration. "Think Before You Ink: Are Tattoos Safe?" Retrieved November 15, 2014 (http://www.fda.gov/ForConsumers/ConsumerUpdates/ucm048919.htm).

WebMD. "Laser Tattoo Removal Procedures, Benefits, and Risks." Retrieved November 25, 2014 (http://www.webmd.com/skin-problems-and-treatments/laser-tattoo-removal).

A

Alliance of Professional Tattooists, 12, 31
antibacterial soap, 4, 55
apprenticeships, 23, 26, 27, 28, 31–35, 36, 37, 39, 44, 65
  costs of, 33
  end of, 36–38
  requirements for, 31
aprons, 41, 47
autoclaves, 41, 47–48

B

bacteria, 46–47
benefits, 17–18, 51, 52, 65
blood, 4, 43, 46, 55
blood-borne diseases, 29, 46–47

C

cardiopulmonary resuscitation (CPR), 31, 46
celebrities, 14, 56, 57
certification, 17, 28, 31, 34, 38, 46, 54, 58–59
code requirements, 48, 61, 62
collaboration, 19–20

community, tattoo studios in a, 18–20, 49
consent, 41, 43
contamination, 15, 43
customers, 4, 6, 14, 15, 17, 18–19, 20, 21–22, 23, 26, 28, 36, 38, 51, 52, 53, 54, 55, 56, 58, 59, 60,
  finding of, 61, 62, 65, 66, 67
  negotiations with, 57–58
  protection of, 6, 39, 41, 43, 49
custom work, 17, 22, 52–53, 57

D

designs of tattoos, 6, 7, 21, 23, 25, 26, 27, 32–33, 34, 50, 52, 53, 57, 58, 67
disinfectants, 48
diversification, 18

E

education
  art, 17, 23, 28
  health safety, 15, 17
  requirements to become a tattoo artist, 29, 31

tattoo schools, 34–35
equipment, 15, 17, 47,
    48, 50, 54, 55

F

face masks, 41, 47
first aid, 29, 31, 39
flash tattoos, 52–53
fungi, 46–47

G

gloves, 4, 41, 47

H

hand tapping, 56
health inspectors, 48–49
hepatitis, 46
history of tattooing, 9,
    12, 54
HIV, 46

I

infections, prevention of,
    4, 15, 17, 29, 39, 47
inks, 4, 7, 41, 43, 54,
    55, 58

J

job, finding a, 38, 52

L

laws, 12, 15, 28, 31, 41,
    43, 47, 48, 49
  zoning, 49, 62
licenses, 6, 17, 21, 39,
    41, 43, 46–50, 65
  fees for getting, 61
  process of getting, 29,
    31, 38

M

mentor, 28, 31, 33, 36,
    37–38
  finding a, 31–35, 37
minors, tattooing of,
    14, 43
Mitchell, Jordan, 44

N

needles, 7, 9, 54, 56

O

Otzi, tattoos of, 10
outline, 4, 55

P

pay for tattoo artists,
    50–53
pigments, 7, 41, 43, 55

placement of tattoos, 21, 52, 57
portfolios, 26, 27, 32, 33, 35–36, 64–65

R

razor, disposable, 4, 55
reputation, 23, 24, 25, 34, 50

S

safety, 12, 17, 20, 48
  regulations, 6, 7, 15, 17, 29, 39, 41, 43, 48, 65
shapes of tattoos, 6
stencil, 4
styles, 22–23, 27, 57, 58
  development of personal, 15, 22, 35–37

T

tattoo expos, 64–65
tattoo machine, 4, 32–33, 36, 47, 48, 54, 55, 56
tattoo removal services, 6, 17, 58–59
tattoo schools, 34–35
tattoo shops, 4, 6, 7, 18, 27, 32–33, 34, 37, 38, 39, 43, 50, 53
  opening own, 17, 61–63, 65–67
  regulations for, 49
techniques, 6, 23, 27, 28, 34, 36, 39, 56
tuberculosis, 46

About the Author

Jason Porterfield has written numerous books for young adults, including several volumes on careers and a book entitled *Tattoos and Secret Societies*. A Chicago-based writer and journalist, Porterfield has been interested in tattooing as an art form since his youth in a college town in southwestern Virginia.

Photo Credits

Designer: Nicole Russo; Editor: Kathy Kuhtz Campbell